Sports Nutrition

for Teen Athletes
Eat Right to Take Your Game to the Next Level

by Dana Meachen Rau

Consultant:
Thomas Inkrott
Head Strength and Conditioning Coach
Minnesota State University, Mankato

CAPSTONE PRESS
a capstone imprint

Sports Illustrated Kids Sports Training Zone is published by Capstone Press,
1710 Roe Crest Drive, North Mankato, Minnesota 56003.
www.capstonepub.com

Books published by Capstone Press are manufactured with paper
containing at least 10 percent post-consumer waste.

Library of Congress Cataloging-in-Publication Data
Rau, Dana Meachen, 1971–
    Sports nutrition for teen athletes : eat right to take your game to the next level / by Dana Meachen Rau.
        p. cm.—(Sports illustrated kids. sports training zone.)
    Includes bibliographical references and index.
    ISBN 978-1-4296-7681-6 (library binding)
    ISBN 978-1-4296-8000-4 (paperback)
    1. Teenage athletes—Nutrition—Juvenile literature. I. Title. II. Series.
    TX361.A8R38 2012
    617.1'027083—dc23   2011033557

Editorial Credits
Anthony Wacholtz, editor; Heidi Thompson, designer; Eric Gohl, media researcher;
    Marcy Morin, scheduler; Laura Manthe, production specialist

Photo Credits
Alamy: Angela Hampton Picture Library, 32, Corbis Bridge, 35, Jochen Tack, 37; Capstone
Studio: Karon Dubke, 18–19, 26–27, 36, 38–39, 40–41; Getty Images: Olaf Tiedje, 20;
iStockphoto: Alberto Pomares, 22, GMVozd, 12, Kristian Sekulic, 33, Prokhorov, design
element (backgrounds); Newscom: Image of Sport, 24, ZUMA Press, 25; Shutterstock: Amy
Myers, 45, Apollofoto, cover (bottom middle left), Benis Arapovic, cover (bottom middle
right), Dirk Ott, cover (bottom left), Elena Gaak, 15, Monkey Business Images, cover
(bottom middle & bottom right), 30, 31, Warren Goldswain, cover (top), Wavebreakmedia
Ltd, back cover, 14, 17; Sports Illustrated: Al Tielemans, 8 (top), 11, Bill Frakes, 5, Bob
Martin, 7, 8 (bottom), Damian Strohmeyer, 4, Heinz Kluetmeier, 10, John Iacono, 42, John
W. McDonough, 9, 21, 28, Robert Beck, 13, 16, Simon Bruty, 6, 23, 29, 34, 43, 44

Acknowledgements
Special thanks to Andrea Buono, B.S. Exercise Physiology and Nutrition, M.A. Nutrition,
for her careful review of this manuscript, and to Ericka Fangiullo, Physical Education/
Health Teacher, Windsor High School, Connecticut; Sharon McHale, Clinical Exercise
Physiologist; and Aubrey Schulz, Holistic Health Coach, for sharing their input and expertise.

Printed in the United States of America in North Mankato, Minnesota.
062012   006747R

TABLE of CONTENTS

chapter 1   FUEL THE FIRE   4

chapter 2   NUTRIENT NEWS   10

chapter 3   THE FUNCTION OF FLUIDS   20

chapter 4   IMPROVE YOUR PERFORMANCE   28

chapter 5   THE RIGHT WAY TO BUILD YOUR BODY   42

GLOSSARY   46

READ MORE   47

INTERNET SITES   47

INDEX   48

Fuel the Fire

A hockey player zigzags across the ice to an open goal. A cross-country runner pushes through the last mile of her race. A gymnast focuses on the beam for the dismount. For all sports, whether on rinks, roads, mats, fields, courts, or slopes, you need **energy**.

After a grueling practice or game, you might collapse in the grass. You and your teammates might moan that you're out of energy. And you're right. Playing sports uses up energy.

A campfire needs logs, branches, or paper to keep burning. The flames go out when the fire runs out of its energy source. Just like a fire, your body burns fuel. You have to feed the fire inside you with food.

Expert Advice

"Your body is like a car," physical education and health teacher Ericka Fangiullo tells her students. "You can't drive a car with just any type of fuel, or it will break down. You need to give it gas, and oil, and regularly get it tuned up. For you to stay healthy, you need to feed your body right as well. This includes healthy eating, getting all your nutrients, drinking lots of water, and exercising every day! Don't let your 'car' break down!"

NHL LEFT WING ALEX OVECHKIN

Your body is made of trillions of cells, including red blood cells, skin cells, nerve cells, and muscle cells. Your cells need **nutrients** to do their jobs. Nutrients provide the materials to make energy, build tissues, and help cells work. You need enough nutrients from food to keep your body nourished.

ENERGY—ABILITY TO DO WORK

NUTRIENTS—SUBSTANCES FOUND IN A VARIETY OF FOODS THAT YOUR BODY NEEDS TO FUNCTION

Cells use energy in various ways depending on the type of exercise. There are two main types of exercise: aerobic and anaerobic.

Aerobic means "with oxygen." Anaerobic means "without oxygen." Aerobic activities are sports that keep your heart pumping over a long period of time. They have steady or continuous movement. For these sports, your cells use oxygen to break down molecules of food and release energy.

Anaerobic activities are sports with short bursts of energy, such as track or gymnastics. For these, cells release energy without using oxygen. But your body still needs oxygen during anaerobic activities. You still need to breathe!

U.S. OLYMPIC GYMNAST SHAWN JOHNSON

FACT: Every time you run, jump, or play a sport, you are using the first law of thermodynamics. The law states that energy changes form, but it cannot be created or destroyed. The energy you get from food becomes the energy you use to do your sport.

SPIETH

There's a wide variety of sports you can do for aerobic or anaerobic activities. Many sports are a mix of aerobic and anaerobic exercise.

Aerobic Activities

biking
dancing
hiking
ice skating
rock climbing
rollerblading
rowing

running
skateboarding
skiing
snowboarding
surfing
swimming

Anaerobic Activities

golf
gymnastics
martial arts
tennis

track and field events
volleyball
weight lifting
wrestling

Aerobic and Anaerobic Activities

baseball
basketball
field hockey
football

hockey
lacrosse
soccer
softball

No matter what sport you do, you need nutrients. As an athlete, your body works harder than a less active teenager. So you may need even more nutrients. Let's look at which nutrients your body needs to fuel your fire and help you perform your best.

Chapter 2

Nutrient News

How does your body turn food into fuel? Scientists measure how much energy there is in a food with **calories**. Your body needs a certain number of calories to function normally. And since you're a teen, your body is still growing, so it needs calories for that too. The number of calories you need depends on your age, size, gender, and the type of activities you do. If you do a high-intensity or long-lasting sport, you may need even more calories. The calories come from nutrients, which are divided into six main groups: carbohydrates, protein, fat, vitamins, minerals, and water.

U.S. Olympic swimmer Elizabeth Beisel

CALORIES——MEASUREMENT OF THE AMOUNT
OF ENERGY THAT FOOD GIVES YOU

Carbohydrates

Carbohydrates are the main source of energy for fuel. They are food for the brain too. Your body turns carbohydrates into a simple sugar called **glucose**. In the cell oxygen combines with glucose. It releases energy that gets stored as ATP (adenosine triphosphate). The energy stored in ATP is used up quickly when you use your muscles.

Tracking Your Calories

Your body needs calories, but you need to get the right ones. Experts recommend that your calories should come from:

- Carbohydrates 50%
- Protein 25–30%
- Fat 25–30%

GLUCOSE——SUGAR THAT YOUR CELLS USE TO MAKE ENERGY

Your body might turn glucose into glycogen, a stored form of glucose that your body keeps in your muscles and liver. Carbohydrates also help your body balance its water and salt levels and help proteins and fats work effectively.

Proteins

You are a body builder. That doesn't mean you have huge rippling muscles and spend all your time in the weight room. It means that as you grow, your body is constantly building itself. To do this, you need protein, which repairs, builds, and helps muscle tissue move. It's also used as a source of energy. Proteins are formed from **amino acids**. Your body needs about 20 types of amino acids. It can make some of them itself, but it needs to get others from food. They are called essential amino acids.

FACT: Are you eating too many or too few calories? Your weight is a good measure of calorie intake. Eat too many, and you'll gain weight. Eat too few, and your body will burn its stored fat and you'll lose weight. Active kids need between 2,000 and 3,000 calories a day.

Fats

Your cells use fats for energy and to build brain and nerve tissue. Fats keep you warm and make you feel full after eating. They protect your organs. Fats also help the body absorb vitamins A, D, E, and K. Your body stores fat in various places around your body.

SOME FISH, SUCH AS SALMON, ARE A GOOD SOURCE OF OMEGA-3 FATTY ACIDS. THESE FATTY ACIDS CAN HELP LOWER THE RISK OF HEART DISEASE, CANCER, AND OTHER HEALTH CONDITIONS.

AMINO ACID—A BASIC BUILDING BLOCK OF PROTEIN

Vitamins and Minerals

Vitamins are natural chemicals in foods. Your body makes some vitamins itself. For example, it makes vitamin D from sunlight that reaches your skin. But your body needs to get other vitamins from foods.

'05

Are Energy Bars Good for Kids?

Energy bars are packed with a lot of sugar for energy, as well as protein, vitamins, and fat. They were created for endurance athletes who practice their sports for hours and need to replenish their energy supply. Most kids and teens like you aren't biking, running, or staying on the field that long. Bars shouldn't be used as a replacement for a meal or a snack. In fact, too much protein isn't good for kids. Nutrition expert Andrea Buono says, "Stay away from high-sugared foods or things that come in wrappers." Instead, try to get your fuel from homemade snacks. Try making your own energy bars so you know exactly what you're putting into your body. (See recipe on page 18.)

Vitamin A helps your vision. All B vitamins provide or release energy. Vitamin C binds cells together. Your body can't get all the vitamins it needs from just one food. That's why it's important to have a variety of colorful foods in your diet.

Minerals are natural chemicals that your body can't make on its own. These include calcium and iron. Calcium helps build strong bones. Iron carries oxygen in the blood and helps release it into cells.

Awesome Energy Bars

Life gets busy. You may feel as if you're constantly on the go between school, practice, and homework. Sometimes you need a snack you can tuck in your backpack or take in the car. Don't go hungry between meals or before or after exercise. Take a little time on the weekend to make these energy bars to eat for the rest of the week.

INGREDIENTS

½ cup white flour
½ cup whole wheat flour
¼ cup quick oats
1 teaspoon baking powder
1 egg lightly beaten
⅓ cup honey
⅓ cup almond butter (or any nut butter)
1 teaspoon vanilla extract
2 tablespoons melted butter or margarine
1 tablespoon fat-free milk or soy milk
¼ cup dried fruit (such as raisins, cranberries, or cherries)
¼ cup mini semisweet chocolate chips
¼ cup chopped walnuts
¼ cup sunflower or pumpkin seeds

STEPS

1. Preheat oven to 350°F.
   Grease an 8 x 8-inch baking pan.

2. In a small bowl, combine the flours, oats, and baking powder. In a large bowl, mix the egg, honey, nut butter, vanilla, butter, and milk with a rubber spatula until smooth. Add in the flour mixture. Stir to combine.

3. Stir in the dried fruit, chocolate chips, walnuts, and sunflower seeds.

4. Press the mixture into the baking pan. Bake for 25 minutes or until a toothpick inserted in center comes out clean. Cut into rectangles. Makes eight.

Chapter 3

The Function of Fluids

Perspiration helps your body cool down when you're hot. The more you push your body, the more you sweat. And if it's a really hot day, you'll probably sweat even when you're just waiting on the sidelines.

When you sweat, your body loses water. And you can't live without water. In fact, if you were lost in a hot blazing desert, you would die from lack of water before you'd die from lack of food. More than half your body weight is water. It makes up a major part of your blood. It gets rid of waste as urine. It helps lubricate your joints and body systems, keeps your temperature at a set level, and gives you energy. If you don't keep your water level in a safe range, you'll become **dehydrated**.

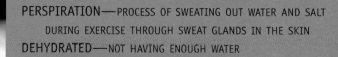

NBA FORWARD
KEVIN DURANT

PERSPIRATION—PROCESS OF SWEATING OUT WATER AND SALT
DURING EXERCISE THROUGH SWEAT GLANDS IN THE SKIN
DEHYDRATED—NOT HAVING ENOUGH WATER

When should you drink? It's simple: Before, during, and after your practice or game. A few hours before you step out on the field, drink a few glasses of water. You can also get water from foods you eat, such as fruits and vegetables. You may not have to worry about dehydration if you're not on the field or court the whole time during a game. But keep a water bottle handy on the sidelines. Nutrition expert Andrea Buono has some advice: "Water is the best for hydrating your body. If it's a hot day, fill the bottle with ice to keep the water cold, and help keep you cool too."

Heat Exhaustion

If you are exposed to heat for too long, and you lose a lot of water through sweat, you could suffer from heat exhaustion. You might feel nauseous, dizzy, weak, or have a headache. Your skin will feel cool and your muscles might cramp up. Heat exhaustion can lead to heat stroke, which starts affecting your brain and nervous system. Tell your coach, parent, or other adult right away or seek medical help! If you're playing in the sun, wear light clothing made of fabrics designed to help heat escape off your skin. Wear a brimmed hat to protect your head. Drink plenty of fluids. If you start feeling dizzy or weak, stop playing. Get yourself into the shade or an air-conditioned building.

During the game drink about five to nine ounces of water every 20 minutes. One ounce equals about two big gulps. After the game continue drinking, especially on hot days or if you feel thirsty.

While you sweat, your body releases electrolytes, which are sodium, magnesium, and potassium. The longer you work out, the more electrolytes your body loses. After most workouts water should do the trick to rehydrate you. But if you have been sweating for 90 minutes or more, sports drinks with electrolytes and carbohydrates can help. Avoid any sports drinks with caffeine.

U.S. OLYMPIC SOCCER GOALIE HOPE SOLO

ELECTROLYTE—A SUBSTANCE IN YOUR BODY THAT HELPS NUTRIENTS AND WASTE FLOW IN AND OUT OF CELLS

Your body will tell you if you're not getting enough water. Thirst is the first sign of dehydration. In fact, when you feel thirsty, you're body is already dehydrated. Other symptoms might include dark-colored urine, dry or "cotton" mouth, cramped muscles, and dizziness.

You shouldn't wait to seek medical attention if your symptoms become severe. If you encounter extreme symptoms, such as a racing pulse or vomiting, you will need medical attention. Doctors will give you an IV to shoot fluids directly into your blood.

Are All Fluids Created Equal?

Water is best. Sports drinks can help you after an intense workout. Milk gives your body fluids, calcium, and protein. Soda, however, is just empty calories. Sugar is a carbohydrate, but foods with added sugar, such as soda and some fruit juices, are mostly sugar and no nutrients. They fill you with "empty" calories. The sugar in these drinks may give you a burst of energy. But then you'll "crash" and feel sluggish and dizzy in the middle of your game. Caffeine can make you more alert and give you an energy boost. But it can also make you jittery and dizzy.

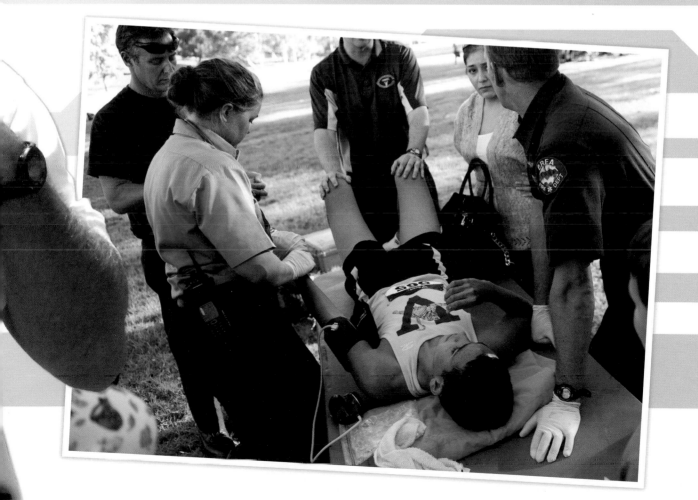

Recovery
Banana Milk Shake

Just four simple ingredients and you can whip
up a sweet, drinkable snack. There are lots
of kinds of milk to use. Soy or almond milk
provides protein like cow's milk. If you're not
a banana fan, make this milkshake with a
handful of fresh berries, peeled peaches,
or juicy pineapple instead.

INGREDIENTS

One ripe banana
2 cups fat-free milk, soy milk,
   or almond milk
¼ teaspoon cinnamon
¼ teaspoon vanilla

STEPS

1. Blend all of the ingredients
in a blender.

2. Pour into a glass, and enjoy as
a post-game recovery drink!

FACT: Bananas are an excellent source of potassium. It can help lower your blood pressure and decrease your chance of a stroke.

Chapter 4

Improve Your Performance

How you eat every day affects how well your body runs on game day. When you have a big athletic event or practice, you're not just pulling on the fuel you just ate. You're pulling from energy that has been building from your overall, healthy diet.

So what are the best power-packed foods to improve your performance? The carbohydrates you need for energy can come from grains. Corn, wheat, rice, and oats are grains that are made into breads, pastas, and crackers. It's best to eat whole grains that have more nutrients, such as whole wheat bread or brown rice, instead of refined grains in white bread and white rice. Starchy vegetables, such as potatoes and peas, also have carbohydrates. The natural sugars in fruit are a burst of carbohydrate energy too.

NFL QUARTERBACK
TOM BRADY

TENNIS STAR
RAFAEL NADAL

REFINED—DESCRIBES FOOD THAT HAS HAD SOME
NUTRIENTS TAKEN OUT

Meat and poultry are packed with protein. Lower fat meats are best. Fish and eggs are filled with protein too. There are tons of plant-based proteins to choose from, such as soy, beans, and nuts.

Dairy foods contain calcium—that means milk, yogurt, and cheese. Some dairy products can be high in fat, so look for low-fat versions. You can also find calcium in spinach, broccoli, beans, almonds, and cereals and juices fortified with calcium. Vegetables have a lot of vitamins, and some have calcium. You can find iron in leafy green vegetables, such as spinach, and in lean red meats. As for fats, try to get them from healthy, nutritious foods, such as nuts, avocados, olives, and fish. Try to stay away from saturated fat in butter, animal meat, or fried foods.

Expert Advice

Athletes should "try to eat a rainbow of colors" when they decide which fruits and vegetables to eat, says holistic health coach Aubrey Schulz. Fruits and vegetables do come in a lot of colors. Apples can be red or yellow, melons can be pink and green, squashes are yellow or orange. Some colors indicate that a food has certain nutrients stocked inside. For example, orange vegetables, such as carrots and sweet potatoes, have a big dose of beta-carotene. Your body changes beta-carotene into vitamin A, which it uses for vision, healthy skin, and your immune system.

Before the Game

About two to four hours before your practice or game, you should have a meal of mostly carbohydrates, a little protein, and a little fat. By game time the food will be out of your stomach. If you ran out onto the field with a full stomach, your body would have to take blood away from digesting to send to your muscles. If your last meal is right before the game, however, cut out the fat.

If your practice or game is late morning, avoid donuts for breakfast. Instead have cereal, cottage cheese, granola, yogurt, eggs, nut butters, or vegetables and fruit. If your practice or game is after school, be sure to have a good lunch and skip the chips or fatty desserts.

The meal may be enough fuel to keep you going. But there may be a lot of time between your meal and your game. You may want a snack closer to game time, such as a banana, apple, pretzels, bagel, or nuts and raisins. It's not the time for junk food. "If you ate the early lunch period at school, or your team needs to take a bus to the event more than an hour away," says clinical exercise physiologist Sharon McHale, "then nutritious snacks and drinks come in handy. If your stomach is rumbling, your performance may too."

During the Game

During your activity, staying hydrated should be your top priority. Stop at the sidelines for sips of water. Keep a water bottle strapped to your bike if you're on a long ride. Carry a bottle in your backpack if you're hiking. Even swimmers sweat. Just because you're wet from the pool on the outside doesn't mean you don't need water on the inside. Be sure to drink up.

If your exercise lasts more than an hour and a half, sports drinks can help replenish some carbohydrates and electrolytes. But don't just rely on packaged drinks to replace your carbohydrates. Fruit, such as oranges, pears, grapes, melons, and apples, are more natural sources. Fruit is made of water and nutrients, so it can help quench your thirst too. Cut up fruit ahead of time and put servings in zip-top bags. Keep them in your sports bag or backpack. Then when you need a bite, they'll be easy to grab before you head out onto the field.

Don't Be Afraid to Experiment!

Everyone's body is different, so it may take some time for you to figure out the best foods to fuel you for a big game. While you train, try various food combinations to see which ones give you the most energy and best performance. Once you find a mix that works for you, re-create it before a big competition. Don't be afraid to try new foods and keep experimenting!

After the Game

After your team is back in the locker room at the end of the game, you need to refuel the water and energy you lost. Within about a half an hour, hydrate with water or a drink with some carbohydrates and protein. Eat a snack, such as dried fruit or pretzels. If you're extra tired, have a banana. Always keep a snack and water in your sports bag in case you have a long bus or car ride home after the game.

Then about two to four hours later, eat a meal. This meal should have carbohydrates and some protein. You may not feel like having fat, but be sure to have healthy fats later on in the day. These after-game snacks and meals help you rehydrate, repair your muscles, and fill up your glycogen tanks to prepare you for your next activity.

You've been running around, burning through fuel, and your body needs a rest. A meal is an opportunity to sit back, relax, and take a break. Eat slowly, chat with your family and friends, and share the story of a game well played.

Food Thoughts

Try one of these delicious, healthful options for breakfast, lunch, dinner, or a snack.

for breakfast

- Scrambled egg with spinach and a tomato on a whole grain bagel

- Oatmeal topped with apples, raisins, and cinnamon

- Blueberry pancakes topped with yogurt (instead of syrup)

for lunch

- Peanut butter and jelly sandwich on multigrain bread

- Cottage cheese with berries

- Vegetable soup with rice

- Turkey and lettuce wrapped in a whole wheat tortilla

for dinner

- Baked white or sweet potato topped with cheese and broccoli

- Pasta with Parmesan cheese and steamed vegetables

- Grilled chicken with brown rice and mixed vegetables

for snacks

- Bananas dipped in yogurt

- Apples and any nut butter

- Trail mix of nuts, dried fruit, and cereal

- Grapes and a cheese stick

- Popcorn or pretzels (without butter or salt)

Yogurt Sundae

You've probably heard your parents, coaches, and teachers say that breakfast is the most important meal of the day. They're right. Your body wakes up needing fuel. Make sure to start the day with a mix of nutrients. Give this sundae a try to start your morning right.

FACT: Sundaes aren't just for dessert. This yogurt sundae is a mix of carbohydrates, protein, calcium, and healthy fat all in one bowl.

INGREDIENTS

One 6-ounce nonfat vanilla or fruit flavored yogurt
Handful of your favorite whole grain cereal
Handful of ripe berries
Handful of chopped nuts

STEPS

1. Spoon the yogurt into a bowl.

2. Sprinkle the cereal onto the yogurt.

3. Add in the berries and nuts.

4. Stir it all together and dig in!

Chapter 5

The Right Way to Build Your Body

Good food fuels your body. But you might see advertisements or hear rumors about steroids or supplements that go beyond what good food can do. They may sound like an easy way to get strong fast. But your body doesn't need them to help you perform. In fact, they can do some major damage.

Anabolic steroids act like natural **hormones** to build strength, endurance, and muscles. But they have serious side effects and are illegal without a prescription. Some anabolic steroids have been banned by many professional sports.

Anabolic steroids are very addictive. They can keep you from growing taller, make you lose your hair, and put you at a greater risk for heart disease, cancer, and stroke. They can damage your reproductive system and make you feel moody or aggressive. Some side effects may not show up for years after you take them.

JOSE CANSECO WAS A MAJOR LEAGUE SLUGGER WHO LATER ADMITTED TO USING STEROIDS.

FLOYD LANDIS WAS STRIPPED OF HIS 2006 TOUR DE FRANCE VICTORY AFTER TESTING POSITIVE FOR STEROIDS.

HORMONE—SUBSTANCE MADE BY A GLAND IN THE BODY THAT AFFECTS A PERSON'S GROWTH AND DEVELOPMENT

What's the best way to build your body? Training is hard work. There's no easy way out. But doing exercises and practicing skills are the best way to strengthen your muscles and develop endurance. A doctor may suggest you take a multivitamin every day to make sure your body gets what it needs. It's best to get the rest from food.

You're OUT!

The fuel you put in your mouth affects how well you perform—so why would you want to put something in that hurts you? Smoking makes it hard for your lungs to breathe. Over time smoking can cause cancer. Avoid those strikes against you and stay in the game instead.

"Your muscles and fitness are not just made on the field," holistic health coach Aubrey Schulz reminds her athletes. "They're made in the kitchen too." Eat the right balance of nutrients for your body to grow and burn energy. And don't just fuel your sport. Fuel your growing body too.

A fire inside you burns with the thrill of competition, the satisfaction of a well-earned win, and the friendship of teammates who helped get you there. Feed that fire with the best fuel to keep you in the game until the final whistle.

Glossary

aerobic—with oxygen

amino acid—basic building block of protein; amino acids can be made by the body or ingested through eating foods with protein

anaerobic—without oxygen

calorie—measurement of the amount of energy that food gives you

dehydrated—not having enough water

electrolyte—substance in your body that helps nutrients and waste flow in and out of cells

glucose—sugar that your cells use to make energy

glycogen—extra glucose stored in the liver and muscles that is used for backup energy

hormone—substance made by a gland in the body that affects a person's growth and development

nutrients—substances found in a variety of foods that your body needs to function

perspiration—process of sweating out water and salt during exercise through sweat glands in the skin

refined—describes food that has had some nutrients taken out

steroids—artificial or natural substances that imitate hormones in the body

Read More

Brancato, Robin F. *Food Choices: The Ultimate Teen Guide.* It Happened to Me. Lanham, Md.: Scarecrow Press, 2010.

Gold, Rozanne. *Eat Fresh Food: Awesome Recipes for Teen Chefs.* New York: Bloomsbury Children's Books, 2009.

Rau, Dana Meachen. *A Teen Guide to Fast, Delicious Lunches.* Teen Cookbooks. Mankato, Minn.: Compass Point Books, 2011.

Shanley, Ellen L., and Colleen A. Thompson. *Fueling the Teen Machine: What It Takes to Make Good Choices for Yourself Every Day.* Boulder, Col.: Bull Publishing Company, 2011.

Internet Sites

FactHound offers a safe, fun way to find Internet sites related to this book. All of the sites on FactHound have been researched by our staff.

Here's all you do:

Visit *www.facthound.com*

Type in this code: 9781429676816

Index

aerobic activities, 6, 8, 9
amino acids, 14, 15
anabolic steroids, 42
anaerobic activities, 6, 7, 8–9
ATP (adenosine triphosphate), 12

banana milk shake recipe, 26–27
beta-carotene, 31
breakfast, 32, 38, 40–41
Buono, Andrea, 16, 22

caffeine, 23, 25
calcium, 17, 25, 31, 40
calories, 10, 12, 14, 25
carbohydrates, 10, 12, 13, 23, 28, 32, 35, 36, 37, 40
cells, 5, 6, 7, 12, 15, 17
clothing, 22

dehydration, 20, 21, 22, 24–25
desserts, 32, 40
dinner, 39

eating schedule, 32–33, 36–37
electrolytes, 23, 35
energy, 4, 5, 6, 7, 10, 12, 14, 15, 16, 17, 18, 20, 25, 28, 36, 45
energy bars, 16, 18–19
essential amino acids, 14

Fangiullo, Ericka, 4
fats, 10, 12, 13, 15, 16, 30, 31, 32, 37, 40
fruits, 22, 25, 28, 31, 32, 35, 36, 38, 39

glucose, 12, 13
glycogen, 13, 37
grains, 28

heat exhaustion, 22

iron, 17, 31

lunch, 32, 33, 38

magnesium, 23
McHale, Sharon, 33
minerals, 10, 17

nutrients, 4, 5, 9, 10, 28, 31, 35, 40, 45

oxygen, 6, 7, 12, 17

perspiration, 20, 21, 22, 23, 34
potassium, 23, 27
proteins, 10, 12, 13, 14, 16, 25, 26, 30, 32, 36, 37, 40

recipes, 18–19, 26–27, 40–41

salt, 13
Schulz, Aubrey, 31, 45
smoking, 44
snacks, 16, 18, 26, 33, 36, 37, 39
soda, 25
sports drinks, 23, 25, 35
sugars, 12, 16, 25, 28
sweat. *See* perspiration

thermodynamics, 7
tissues, 5, 14, 15

vegetables, 22, 28, 31, 32, 38, 39
vitamins, 10, 15, 16–17, 31, 44

water, 4, 10, 13, 20, 22–25, 34, 35, 36
weight, 14, 20

yogurt sundae recipe, 40–41